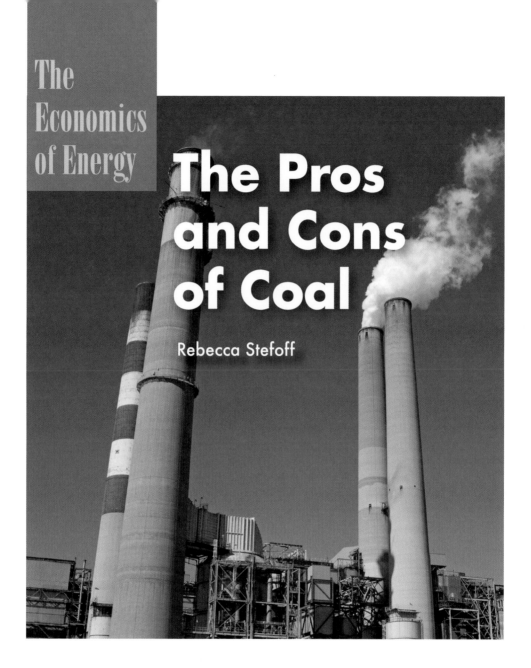

The Economics of Energy

The Pros and Cons of Coal

Rebecca Stefoff

Cavendish Square

New York

Published in 2015 by Cavendish Square Publishing, LLC
243 5th Avenue, Suite 136, New York, NY 10016

Library of Congress Cataloging-in-Publication Data
Stefoff, Rebecca, 1951- author.
The pros and cons of coal / Rebecca Stefoff.
     pages cm. — (The economics of energy)
Includes bibliographical references and index.
ISBN 978-1-62712-918-3 (hardcover) ISBN 978-1-62712-920-6 (ebook)
1. Coal—Economic aspects—Juvenile literature. 2. Coal—Environmental aspects—Juvenile literature. I. Title.

TN801.S74 2015
333.8'22—dc23

2014005290

Editorial Director: Dean Miller
Editor: Kristen Susienka
Senior Copy Editor: Wendy A. Reynolds
Art Director: Jeffrey Talbot

Designer: Amy Greenan
Production Manager: Jennifer Ryder-Talbot
Production Editor: David McNamara
Photo Researcher: J8 Media

Printed in the United States of America

The Economics of Energy

Table of Contents

Loaded with coal, a train passes through Wyoming on its way to a shipping port in the Pacific Northwest. A growing percentage of U.S. coal is exported.

Chapter 1

The Black Stone That Burns

Coal is humankind's second most used energy source, after oil. It provides 40 percent of the world's electricity and about 28 percent of the energy used for all purposes around the planet, from heating homes to melting iron ore. Coal powered the Industrial Revolution (1760s–1850s) that gave birth to the modern world. It remains a source of power, profit, and jobs. It is also the cause of deadly mining accidents, toxic chemical spills, and carbon dioxide in the atmosphere that is contributing to global climate change.

Although the benefits and risks of coal use are greater today than they have ever been, people have used coal for several thousand years. The story of coal, however, began long before human life emerged. To understand the pros and cons of coal and its place in the world today, it is necessary to start with its origins hundreds of millions of years ago, in the towering forests of primeval Earth.

Capturing Carbon in Coal

Life on Earth started in the oceans. Around 425 billion years ago, life began to colonize the landmasses in the form of the first plants. By

360 million years ago, the continents were densely covered with vegetation that absorbed energy from sunlight and carbon from the air, just as plants do today.

Most of the plants in those lush early forests, however, became extinct long ago. They included the lepidodendron, which reached heights of more than 150 feet, and the sigillaria, with a short, thick trunk and no branches. Huge ferns and sixty-foot-tall relatives of the modern horsetail also flourished in the forests that became the source of coal.

The period between 360 and 290 million years ago is known as the Carboniferous period. Most of the world's coal originated in the plant life of that time. (There are some younger coal beds, however, including a few that are just a million years old.) As Carboniferous vegetation died, it often ended up being covered by other vegetation or by sand, mud, rock, or oxygen-poor water. Because the process of plant decay requires oxygen, and much of the dead plant matter was deprived of oxygen, the plant matter could not completely decay. Its carbon remained behind. At first, the mass of carbon-rich matter was soggy and spongy. Over time, however, the weight above it increased as well as the pressure on it. Mountains also rose in some places, and other landmasses sank beneath the seas.

The pressure and heat of geological forces slowly turned millions of years' worth of compressed plant matter into something harder: coal. Eventually, layers and seams of carbon-rich coal threaded through the ground beneath the Earth's surface, thickest in the places that had been most lush with plant life during the Carboniferous period. Each cubic foot of coal represented about ten cubic feet of prehistoric vegetation. Within that coal was the stored-up energy of sunlight that had fallen on ancient plants when life was still new to the planet.

Steinkohlenformation II.

1. Zahnfarn (Odontopteris). — 2. Schuppenbaum (Lepidodendron). — 3. Cordaites borassifolia. — 4. Pecopteris cyathea. — 5. Kalamiten. — 6. Sigillaria. — 7. Stigmarienform einer Sigillarie mit Wurzeln im Wasser. — 8. Blattstera von Annularien.

Lush forests that flourished in the Carboniferous period became the coal that is mined today.

Early Uses

The first known human use of coal was in northeastern China around six thousand years ago, when people began carving ornaments from hard, shiny coal. By 1000 BCE, the Chinese were burning coal as fuel. Later, they learned to bake coal slowly to burn out any **impurities** in it, producing a purified form of coal called **coke**. This was useful in ironworking, which required iron ore to be mixed with fuel before being melted. Impurities in coal could contaminate and weaken the iron, but coke was free of this problem. Coke-fueled furnaces allowed the medieval Chinese ironworking industry to expand.

On the other side of the world, in North America, at least one Native American culture began using coal after about 1000 BCE. The Hopi people of the Southwest mined coal and used it for cooking, heating, and firing their clay pottery.

In Europe, the Greek scientist Theophrastes wrote around 300 BCE that metalworkers burned coal to heat their materials and furnaces.

A DEEPER DIVE

Marco Polo and the Many Baths

The Italian traveler Marco Polo, who lived in China for years before returning to his home city of Venice in 1295 CE, became famous for his stories about the things he had seen and done in his journeys across Asia. One of the marvels he described was the black stone that burns:

It is a fact that all over the country of Cathay [China] there is a kind of black stones [sic] existing in beds in the mountains, which they dig out and burn like firewood. If you supply the fire with them at night, and see that they are well kindled, you will find them still alight in the morning; and they make such capital fuel that no other is used throughout the country. It is true that they have plenty of wood also, but they do not burn it, because those stones burn better and cost less.

He added that the population of Cathay was "vast," and that everyone took at least three hot baths a week,

Marco Polo may have seen marble baths such as this one photographed in China around 1900.

more in winter. Wood alone could not possibly heat enough water for all those baths, he claimed. Only the "black stones," now known as coal, allowed the Chinese people to maintain their habit of frequent bathing—a habit that seemed outlandish to Europeans of the time.

Several centuries later, Roman soldiers in Britain used coal, which they collected from natural outcroppings, for carving into ornaments and for burning to keep warm. Not until after 1100 CE, though, did Europeans regularly start using coal as fuel. Some of the earliest accounts of coal use come from Britain, which had large deposits of coal and would eventually develop not just a thriving trade in the resource but also new industries based on it.

Needed: A New Fuel

By the twelfth century CE, Europe had a pressing need for a new fuel. For thousands of years people had used three traditional fuels: wood, charcoal, and **peat**. Like coal, these are plant-based fuels, but they had certain disadvantages.

Wood is the oldest known fuel. Archaeologists now think that our prehuman ancestors may have made wood fires as early as a million years ago. Charcoal is partially burned wood, created by burning wood slowly at a low, smoldering heat with little oxygen, usually by half-burying the wood or enclosing it in an oven. Charcoal burns hotter and with less smoke than wood, and it is lighter and easier to transport. The manufacture of charcoal, however, requires a lot of wood.

The use of wood and charcoal by ancient civilizations led to deforestation, or the loss of trees, in many areas around the Mediterranean Sea and in the Middle East. By the 1100s CE, deforestation was becoming a problem in parts of Europe. The area around London, the largest European city of the time, was largely deforested by 1200, due to the cutting of trees for timber, firewood, and charcoal.

A woodcutter in the Middle Ages fells a tree with his axe. Widespread cutting of forests opened land for farming but created the need for a new fuel source.

The problem was not just that the growing population needed fuel for cooking and heat. The end of the Middle Ages also brought a demand for manufactured goods such as glass windows and metal utensils. Workshop-scale industries, including glassmaking, blacksmithing, and the smelting of metals, consumed ever-growing amounts of charcoal. Peat was not the answer.

English peat gatherers at work in 1905, stacking plant matter cut from a bog to be dried and burned as fuel.

Peat is partially decayed vegetation—usually moss and shrubs—that builds up in wetlands, such as bogs. As plants die, layers of plant matter build up, but it does not decay completely because oxygen is needed for decomposition, and the water in a peat environment is low in oxygen. The incompletely decayed plant matter builds up in dense, compressed layers, forming peat. After peat is cut out in blocks, pressed to squeeze out the water, and allowed to dry, it can be burned as a fuel. People in areas with peat bogs used—and some still do use—peat instead of wood or charcoal for heating and cooking. Peat produces less heat and more ash than charcoal, however, making it unsuitable for industrial use.

Coal met the rising need for a hot-burning fuel that did not require the cutting of trees. In the thirteenth century, blacksmiths and smelters began burning coal in their workshops and foundries. However, people did not burn coal for domestic uses, such as cooking and heating their homes. The burning of coal produced so much smoke and such a disagreeable smell that it was considered too disgusting for home use. Still, it was not long before so much coal was being used for business and industrial purposes in London and other cities that people complained of the soot, smoke, and stench. King Edward I took action in 1306, banning the use of coal altogether.

The ban failed. The need for fuel was too great. By the late sixteenth century people were burning coal in their homes, thanks to a new trend in domestic architecture: the chimney, which funneled smoke up and away. As more and more buildings were built with chimneys, people became willing to enjoy the heat and energy of coal in their homes—while also adding to the amount of coal smoke in the atmosphere overhead. By 1700, an English writer named Timothy Nourse would say about London that, "of all the Cities perhaps in Europe, there is not a more nasty and a more unpleasant Place," because of coal smoke.

Powering the Industrial Revolution

At first, most of the coal used in Britain came from the area around the city of Newcastle on the Tyne River. People could simply pick up loose

A DEEPER DIVE

A Mine Ahead of Its Time

In 1590, Sir George Bruce of Carnock built an ingenious new mine to get at a coal seam that ran beneath the Firth of Forth, an arm of the sea in Scotland. Bruce sent workers out at low tide to build an artificial island on the floor of the firth. It took the form of a wide, circular, forty-foot-tall tower or shaft, made of huge stones sealed with clay to keep out water when the tide flowed back into the firth. Inside, miners could tunnel down into the coal seam. Outside, cargo ships could float at high tide to load the coal. King James VI of Scotland was so impressed when he visited the mine that he knighted Bruce. Unfortunately, a mighty storm and a high spring tide destroyed the shaft and flooded the mine in 1625. Today, all that remains of Bruce's bold venture is a pile of rocks visible at low tide.

This pump, installed in a coal mine in Rutherglen, Scotland in the 1730s, was one of the first to use Newcomen's new steam engine. The engine ran on coal and made mines more productive.

coals that fell from cliffs and outcroppings. Soon, though, workers began digging into the hills to get more coal. Mines developed around Newcastle, and then in other parts of Britain and Europe. As time went on, miners had to go deeper to obtain coal, and flooding—from river, rain, sea, or ground water—became a problem in many mines.

The solution was pumping. Early pumps were powered by men or horses, but an ironworker named Thomas Newcomen had a better idea. His Newcomen engine, as it was called, was first used to pump water out of a coal mine in 1712. A boiler filled with water was heated by burning coal until the water turned to steam. The steam passed into a metal cylinder, and then cold water was added to the cylinder to drop the temperature and cause the steam to condense into more water. Since the water took up less space than the steam, the condensation created a vacuum in the cylinder. The vacuum sucked a sliding **piston** down into the cylinder, and then the process was repeated. The up-and-down movement of the piston drove the pump that drained water from the mine.

James Watt of Scotland, shown in a 1792 portrait, has been called the Father of the Industrial Revolution for his work perfecting a highly efficient steam engine.

Newcomen's engines were simple coal-fired steam engines. Before long they would transform industry—and the world.

One of Newcomen's engines could do as much work as fifty horses, but the engines required enormous amounts of coal. This was not a problem when they were used at coal mines, but it prevented them from being used elsewhere. Not until Scotsman James Watt developed a more efficient steam engine in the 1770s did this revolutionary device reach its full potential. Watt's engine got four times as much energy from a piece of coal as Newcomen's.

Around the same time, the British mastered the technology of purifying coal into large quantities of coke that could be used in the making of high-quality iron. Many industries, including textile mills and glassworks, had already switched from earlier sources of power, such as charcoal or waterwheels, to coal. Now the iron industry could do so as well. The combination of coal, iron, and the steam engine gave birth to the transformation known as the Industrial Revolution.

For years, horses had pulled loaded carts away from Britain's coal mines on iron rails, which let the carts run more smoothly than they would run over the ground. Before long, though, Watts's coal-fired steam engine was harnessed to a locomotive that could pull more carts than a team of horses, and the railroad industry was born.

The first railroad ran for twenty-six miles from a coal mine to a river port where the coal was loaded onto ships. In 1830, a train linked the British manufacturing cities of Manchester and Liverpool; the first train on that route reached the dizzying speed of thirty-five miles per hour. By 1845, Britain had built 2,200 miles of railroads. Seven years later, that figure had jumped to more than 6,000. Railroads grew even faster

The opening of the Liverpool and Manchester Railway in 1830 caused a sensation. People had not dreamed it was possible to travel at thirty-five miles per hour.

after 1855, when Henry Bessemer patented a new method of using coke to produce steel, which is iron with a specific carbon content that makes it harder, easier to shape, and more durable than other kinds of iron. Steel railroad tracks began spreading like nerve networks through many nations, speeding the travel of passengers and the transport of goods.

Steel also made possible the construction of large coal-fired steamships and of a new kind of building, the skyscraper.

Since the late 1700s people had been using coal to create artificial light. When heated, coal gives off flammable gases that can be contained and used for illumination. This meant that labor was no longer tied to the rhythms of natural light and darkness. Coal-gas lights enabled the new factories to operate twenty-four hours a day. After 1882, when American inventor and businessman Thomas Edison opened the first electric power plant—using coal as fuel and serving part of New York City—electric lights became the standard. More and more coal was needed to fuel the power plants that sprang up.

The Industrial Revolution was powered by coal. At the same time, it increased the demand for coal. It brought sweeping technological, economic, and social changes, including the shift toward a more urban world. As industrialization spread, the rise in the number of factories and factory jobs drew people in Britain and other countries from the countryside to the city. The large-scale manufacture of heavy machinery and many other kinds of equipment and consumer goods; the construction of new and bigger trains, ships, and buildings; and the world's growing reliance on electricity all grew out of the need for an engine to pump water out of coal mines.

Mines and Miners

To meet the growing hunger for coal, mine owners and operators had to do two things: open new mines, and get more coal out of existing mines. In Britain, coal was abundant in central and northern England, Scotland,

and Wales. During the eighteenth and nineteenth centuries, many new mines were opened in those regions, while existing mines expanded with deeper and more extensive tunnels and shafts. The nineteenth century brought an expansion of coal mining in North America, Australia, Japan, India, South Africa, Russia, and more than a dozen nations in Europe.

In some regions, such as Wales in Britain and Pennsylvania and West Virginia in the United States, coal was mined in remote, hilly areas far from major population centers. The mines offered employment, and in some areas it was common for several generations of men in each family to work in the mines, and for coal mining to be the occupation of almost the entire population. Conditions in most mines, however, were dismal at best. Miners worked long hours with picks, axes, and shovels—mining did not begin to be mechanized until the twentieth century. Some employers paid miners with special "scrip," or written documents, instead of money. The scrip could only be exchanged for merchandise at a store owned by the mining company, which often charged inflated prices for food and other goods. The labor force at many mines included children. In Britain, a parliamentary commission that investigated child labor in the 1840s found that children as young as five years old often worked twelve-hour shifts in darkness deep in the coal mines, operating the trap doors that controlled air circulation.

In addition to overwork and the danger of accidents, miners faced health risks. Many suffered from a disease called "black lung," now known as coalworker's pneumoconiosis, caused by inhaling coal dust. Even children who did not work in the mines felt their effects. In heavily industrialized British cities such as Manchester, many young people suffered from rickets, a condition that causes weakness and deformity of the bones.

Coal workers—like these men standing with a fossil palm leaf found in a Colorado mine in 1907—performed dangerous jobs to feed the world's appetite for fuel.

A DEEPER DIVE

The Three Deadly "Damps"

Early coal miners faced many dangers below ground. Among the deadliest were three gases that seventeenth century English miners started calling "damps," possibly from the German word *dampf*, meaning "fog" or "vapor."

"Choke damp" was the term for what we now know as carbon dioxide, which is released when long-buried coal is exposed to oxygen. In a place with poor air circulation, such as a tunnel, carbon dioxide gathers in pools. Someone who enters a pocket of this invisible gas can suffocate in moments.

"White damp"—which is invisible, not white—is another odorless gas, carbon monoxide. It is a by-product of incomplete combustion, or burning. It was most commonly found in mines after a fire or explosion, and could suffocate people who were trying to rescue injured miners.

Most dreaded of all was "fire damp," or methane. True to its name, this "damp" is highly flammable. It forms

part of the fuel known as natural gas, which, like coal, is a product of partially decayed plant matter. Methane is lighter than air. When released from cracks in coal seams, it floats up and gathers beneath the ceilings of mine tunnels. A candle, lantern, or spark could instantly ignite the methane, with explosive results.

Miners eventually adopted the practice of lowering a canary into the shaft of a coal mine before going down themselves. If the bird dropped from its perch, the miners knew that it had been killed by gas. Before canaries came into wide use, miners sometimes used dogs for the same purpose, although a 1662 document from one mine reports that the operators would not use a dog until after the first miner to be lowered had died.

A miner in India in 2013 carries coal hundreds of feet up wooden ladders from a deep mine shaft.

Rickets strikes children who do not receive enough vitamin D from sunlight, which was rare in the coal-smoke gloom of factory and mill towns. Barbara Reese wrote in *Coal: A Human History* (2003), "In the new industrial cities, rickets reached epidemic proportions among urban children, and came to be known elsewhere simply as 'the English disease.'" By the 1860s, though, some American cities were just as bad. Pittsburgh, Pennsylvania, may have been the worst. When British traveler Anthony Trollope visited Pittsburgh he described its "filth and wondrous blackness," and said, "The city itself is buried in a dense black cloud."

While industrial cities struggled with coal pollution, the miners who scraped the coal out of the ground were banding together to seek better working conditions and pay.

In Britain, Canada, and the United States, in particular, strikes by coal miners' unions were a major part of the broader labor movement of the late nineteenth and early twentieth centuries. The labor movement eventually led to improved conditions and pay for workers in many industries, and to the rise of labor unions as a political force.

By the early years of the twenty-first century, the nature of coal mining had changed dramatically—at least in some countries. While much mining in India, for example, is still done the old-fashioned way— by individual workers with picks and shovels—nations such as the United States, Germany, Canada, and Australia have highly mechanized their mining operations. China, one of the world's biggest producers and users of coal, has both many large, modern, high-technology mines and thousands of smaller, labor intensive ones. Meanwhile, the United States is one of several coal-producing countries that have begun investigating new technologies aimed at creating cleaner energy from coal. The debate over coal's place in the energy future of America and the world focuses on both the promises and the problems of this ancient fuel.

CRITICAL THINKING

- Coal is a **fossil fuel**. Can you explain why?

- What are the connections between a growing population and the increased demand for fuel?

- How did the demand for coal lead to the Industrial Revolution? How did the Industrial Revolution increase the demand for coal?

A hose carries liquid carbon dioxide away from the coal-fired Schwarze Pumpe power plant in Germany. The carbon dioxide will be pumped into the ground in a technique called carbon capture and storage.

Chapter 2

Advantages of Coal-Based Energy

Coal, now primarily used in the United States to generate electricity at power plants, is part of an energy mix that includes two other fossil fuels—oil and natural gas—along with nuclear power and **renewable energy** sources such as solar, wind, and hydropower. Coal has distinct advantages. It is the least expensive source of energy. It does not explode like natural gas or spill like oil (although gases in coal mines can explode, and chemicals used in connection with coal-processing can spill). To reduce pollution from the burning of coal, a variety of **clean coal technologies (CCT)** can be used. Perhaps coal's chief advantage as a fuel source, however, is that it is abundant, especially in the United States.

Vast Reserves of Energy

The World Coal Association (WCA) estimates that the world has more than 861 billion tons of proven coal **reserves**. (A reserve is the amount of a resource that can be obtained using known technology; a proven reserve is a reserve that has been tested by drilling.) According to the WCA, at current rates of coal production the world's proven reserves are sufficient to meet its energy needs for about 112 years, compared with forty-six years for proven reserves of oil and fifty-four years for natural gas. The United States, China, Russia, and India have the largest proven reserves of coal.

The United States is a coal-rich nation. In 2013, the U.S. Energy Information Administration (EIA) reported that the proven reserves of coal in the United States total 481 billion tons, more than its known reserves of oil or natural gas. Half of that reserve base may be unrecoverable, however, which means that it cannot be mined because of property rights, challenges posed by local geography and geology, and environmental restrictions. The EIA estimated that the nation's recoverable coal reserves total about 257 billion tons.

Recoverability depends on the type of mining operation used to extract the coal. In general, a greater percentage of a reserve can be recovered from a surface mine than from an underground mine. One reason for this is that in underground mining, large pillars of coal are often left in place, rather than being extracted, in order to prevent the ground above the mine from collapsing. Recovery rates can run as high as 90 percent or more at some surface mines, and as low as 40 percent at some underground mines.

Energy Self-Sufficiency

In 2013, the U.S. Department of Energy announced that the United States had produced 84.5 percent of the energy it consumed during the first nine months of the year. Looked at another way, during that period the United States had relied on imported energy for just over 15 percent of its needs and had achieved 84.5 percent energy self-sufficiency. This was the highest energy self-sufficiency the United States had achieved since

1987, up from a low point of 70 percent in 2005.

Coal did not contribute to the sharp rise in America's energy self-sufficiency from 2005 to 2013. The major contributors were oil and natural gas, extracted from reserves in the United States through the use of new techniques such as horizontal drilling and hydraulic fracturing, or fracking. The International Energy Agency predicts that the boom in shale oil production thanks to these techniques could make the United States the world's top producer of oil by 2016, displacing Saudi Arabia. Some projections show the United States becoming 100 percent energy self-sufficient by 2020.

In hydraulic fracturing, or fracking, liquid is pumped into the ground to release natural gas or oil.

Total energy self-sufficiency has long been a goal of many American politicians and planners. It would mean that the energy needed for U.S. economic stability and growth—including such basic needs as heating and the transport of food and other goods—could be supplied entirely from domestic sources. The country would not be at the mercy of strikes, shutdowns, and price variations in other nations that might affect the

A DEEPER DIVE

Types of Coal Mining Operations

Modern coal mining is divided into two basic categories: surface and underground. Each category includes a variety of methods for getting coal out of the ground with the use of heavy machinery. The choice of method for a particular mine depends on the size and depth of the coal seam to be mined, the features of the geography, and environmental concerns and regulations.

Surface mining is used when coal seams are within 200 feet of the surface, although some surface mines in the American West are deeper. In surface mining, heavy equipment is used to scrape away the **overburden**, or soil and rock above the coal. The three main types of surface mining used in the United States are strip mining, auger mining, and mountaintop removal. In strip mining, the overburden is removed in long bands or strips.

In auger mining, the overburden is cut away from a hillside so that coal can be removed from within the hill by huge drill-like machines called augers. In mountaintop removal mining, entire mountaintops are removed to expose coal seams, and the overburden is disposed of in neighboring valleys.

Underground mining removes coal from deeper seams. It involves digging or blasting a shaft or tunnel either into a slope or straight down into the ground, then excavating a network of tunnels along the seam or seams. Coal is removed from its bed by scraping, digging, or blasting before being hauled out of the mine by systems of conveyors and elevators. Modern industrial underground mines make extensive use of remote-controlled equipment, such as roof supports with hydraulic legs to prevent cave-ins. In both surface and underground mining, much of the actual work of scraping, digging, and loading coal can be done by machines, but miners are still needed to operate machinery and to perform tasks that machines cannot execute. In the United States, almost twice as much coal was taken from surface mines in 2012 as from underground mines.

availability of energy. Energy self-sufficiency could have broader effects as well. With no need to depend on oil from the Middle East, for example, America's involvement in the politics of that region might change course. If the United States can meet its energy needs by increasing domestic oil and natural gas production, will the drive to develop economical sources of green or renewable energy be affected?

Although coal is not currently responsible for the increase in America's energy self-sufficiency, the nation's coal reserves are greater than its reserves of oil and natural gas. If total energy self-sufficiency is achieved and becomes an ongoing top priority, coal may be called upon to make a larger contribution. However, because another long-term goal for the United States is the transition into a lower-carbon future, in which energy production releases less carbon into the atmosphere, the focus will be on what government and the energy industry term "clean coal."

Toward Clean Coal

When coal combusts, or burns, a variety of pollutants are released into the air: particles of ash and soot (flecks of burned carbon), mercury, and gases such as sulfur dioxide, nitrogen oxides, and carbon dioxide. Sulfur dioxide, one of the primary emissions from coal combustion, forms tiny particles in the atmosphere. It is one of the leading causes of acid rain, a type of damaging precipitation that has been greatly reduced in the U.S. and many other countries since the 1970s, thanks to the introduction of filters, scrubbers in chimneys, and other devices to remove particles and other emissions from coal smoke. Where those existing technologies are used, they have significantly reduced the amount of particulates, mercury, sulfur

A DEEPER DIVE

From Coal to Electricity

Coal is converted to electricity at power plants. Although details of the process vary, the general outline is something like this:

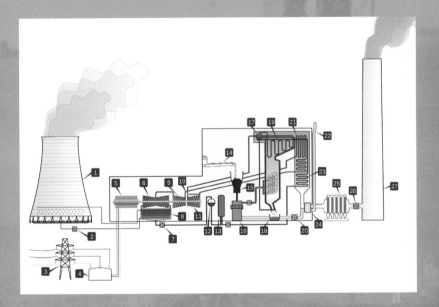

Coal enters this coal-fired power plant on a conveyor (14) and is ground up, mixed with hot air, and sent to a boiler, where it burns. Water in the boiler turns to steam, which drives three turbines (11, 9, and 6). Later, the steam is mixed with water from the cooling tower (1) and returned to the boiler. The gas exhaust from the boiler passes through a cleaner (25) that removes particles, then leaves the plant through the chimney (27).

When completed, Mississippi's Kemper Plant will burn lignite and capture its own emissions.

dioxide, and nitrogen oxides being emitted from coal-burning operations, although they do not capture or remove all pollutants.

Integrated gasification combined cycle (IGCC) technology is one approach to greater reduction of emissions from coal combustion. In an IGCC plant, coal is mixed with steam and oxygen under heat and pressure. This breaks down the coal molecules into gases. Particulates and pollutants can be removed from the coal gases, which are then burned to drive gas-powered turbines, generating energy. Additional energy is produced by the heat of the combustion, which powers steam turbines. Sulfur, hydrogen, and other materials removed from the coal gases can be used in the manufacture of industrial products. The U.S. Department of Energy has built several plants to test IGCC technology, and a commercial plant intended to burn **lignite**, or **brown coal**, using IGCC is under construction in Kemper County, Mississippi.

Particulate pollutants are bad, but a growing amount of scientific evidence indicates that **greenhouse gases**, such as methane and especially carbon dioxide (CO_2), are worse. These gases trap heat in Earth's atmosphere. Human activity—particularly the burning of fossil fuels—is now recognized by the vast majority of scientists to be raising the amount of greenhouse gases and thus causing climate change. The United States and other countries are exploring ways of reducing or limiting carbon emissions, which are likely to come under the same kinds of federal regulations that already govern other pollutants. Currently, coal-burning power plants are the second largest source of CO_2 in the United States, after gasoline-powered vehicles. If coal is to increase its importance in energy's future—or even keep its current place—methods for reducing carbon emissions from coal plants will be essential.

One of the most promising methods is called **carbon capture and storage (CCS)**, which is sometimes also referred to as carbon capture and sequestration. In this process, CO_2 and other greenhouse gases are removed from the exhaust of coal combustion and prevented from entering the atmosphere. The captured gases can then be turned into liquids or solids, injected into neutral media such as saltwater, stored in tanks or underground reservoirs, or some combination of these. Various elements of CCS technology are already in use. In the Sleipner natural gas field off the coast of Norway, for example, a company that is using offshore drilling platforms to extract gas has been piping excess CO_2 from the gas into an

A DEEPER DIVE

The Coal Ranks

Coal takes various forms, depending on the kind of vegetation it is made of, the depth at which it was buried (this determines how much heat and pressure came into play during its formation), and the length of time it has been forming. Geologists and the coal industry classify coal into levels called ranks. Low-rank coals are softer and lower in carbon. High-rank coals are harder and higher in carbon. The higher the rank, the greater the degree of change the original plant material has undergone.

At the bottom of the scale is peat, which is not truly coal but can turn into coal over time. Next comes lignite, which is sometimes called brown or immature coal. Sub-bituminous coal is harder and darker than lignite. **Bituminous** coal is harder and darker still. Hardest and darkest of all is **anthracite**. Bituminous coal and anthracite are considered high-rank coals. With their higher levels of carbon, they contain more stored energy, and therefore produce more heat when burned than lower-rank coals.

Of the coal produced in the United States in 2012, almost 48 percent was bituminous (right), 44 percent was sub-bituminous, nearly 8 percent was lignite (top), and just 0.2 percent was anthracite (below).

A tank to hold carbon dioxide is installed at Schwarze Pumpe, which is intended to serve as a model for larger carbon-capturing coal-fired power plants.

undersea reservoir at the rate of a million tons a year since 1996. The WCA reports that about 32 million tons of CO_2 are already in storage around the world.

The next step is to incorporate CCS technology into full-scale commercial power plants. The small Schwarze Pumpe plant has been operating in Germany since 2008, burning lignite to produce steam used by local industry. In 2010, the plant's operators announced that Schwarze Pumpe was capturing nearly 100 percent of its CO_2, which is carried by tanker truck to a depleted natural gas field and injected into the cavities in the ground that once held natural gas. Schwarze Pumpe is expected to serve as a model for a larger plant, also to be built in Germany. In the United States, the Department of Energy is sponsoring FutureGen, a project to refit an existing plant in Illinois with new IGCC and CCS equipment that is projected to capture and store up to 1.3 million tons of CO_2, or 90 percent of the CO_2 that will be produced by the plant, each year. The Schwarze Pumpe and FutureGen projects are intended to demonstrate that low-carbon coal use is achievable and safe. If they succeed, CCS technologies may give coal a brighter future.

CRITICAL THINKING

- What importance might coal have in international trade and politics?

- What are the advantages to a nation of energy self-sufficiency? Can you think of any potential disadvantages?

- How has the coal industry changed since the 1970s?

A postcard depicting a funeral following the 1906 Courrières,
France mining disaster, which killed almost 1,100 miners.

Chapter 3

Disadvantages of Coal-Based Energy

Ancient Roman soldiers once burned lumps of coal to warm themselves during their cold, damp winters on duty in Britain. Today, coal is among the fossil fuels that are associated with a different kind of warming—the climate change that appears to be raising Earth's temperature. In addition to contributing to the overall problem of greenhouse gases, coal has specific disadvantages that balance its advantages. Among these are dangers to mine workers, damage to the environment and human health, and the high cost of making coal cleaner and greener.

Dangerous, Destructive, and Unhealthy

Coal mining has proved deadly to thousands of workers. Among the biggest coal-mining disasters in history are an explosion at Courrières, France, in 1906 that killed 1,099 miners, including a number of child workers, and one in Benxi, China, in 1942 that killed 1,549, making it the largest disaster in coal-mining history. Mining disasters on such a large scale are unlikely to occur today, but accidents, cave-ins, fires, and explosions continue to claim the lives of miners each year.

A DEEPER DIVE

Disasters Below Ground

A 1907 methane explosion at West Virginia's Monongah Mine killed 362 miners. This and other large-scale disasters led to the formation in 1910 of the U.S. Bureau of Mines to oversee safety in the mining industry. (Safety is now overseen by the Mine Safety and Health Administration of the Department of Labor.)

However, mining remains a dangerous occupation, and miners continue to perish. From 1999 to 2009, accidents killed 354 American miners. Ninety percent of the accidents involved just one or two people. In 2006, for example, at the Aracoma Alma Mine No. 1 in West Virginia, two men died after a misaligned conveyor belt caused parts to rub together, which started a fire in the coal dust that had built up in the area. Deadly carbon monoxide formed, but by the time the alarm was raised, only ten of twelve men working in the deepest part of the mine were able to get out alive.

Federal investigators later found that the water supply to a fire hose had been disconnected, one of the mine's carbon monoxide detectors was missing, and the ventilation system controls were not properly installed, among other safety violations. The company that owned the mine paid $4.2 million in penalties. Four years later, twenty-nine miners died in an explosion at Upper Big Branch, another West Virginia mine owned by the same company.

Mining has killed many people who never set foot inside a mine. In 1966, for example, 112 children and twenty-eight adults were killed when rubble and debris piled outside a coal mine slid downhill and buried a school and other buildings in the village of Aberfan, Wales. Far greater losses, though, have come from the damage done to the environment and to human health by the mining and burning of coal.

"Coal mining destroys land, pollutes thousands of miles of streams and brings massive environmental damage to mountain communities," says the Natural Resources Defense Council. "Pollution from coal plants produces dirty air, acid rain and contaminated land and water. Health problems associated with coal pollution include childhood asthma, birth defects and respiratory diseases that take nearly 25,000 lives each year."

An entire hill is slowly scraped away, one strip at a time, in mountaintop removal mining.

Some 600 landfills and ponds across the United States now store coal waste, much of it contaminated with arsenic, heavy metals, and other toxic materials known to cause diseases, including cancer. These contaminants leak into both ground water and streams. Mining chews up large tracts of land, destroying vegetation, wildlife, and ecosystems. In the decade between 1992 and 2002, surface mining of coal in Appalachia—the coal-rich region that includes eastern Pennsylvania, West Virginia, and parts of several other states—damaged 380,000 acres of forest and 1,000 miles of streams.

Coal attacks human health in several ways. Soot and other particulate pollutants directly affect lung health in people who breathe air contaminated with them. They cause asthma, contribute to heart attacks, and in the case of coal workers, may result in severe lung disease. Furthermore, the mercury that is emitted from coal plants into the atmosphere later settles on land and sea and finds its way into the environment, including drinking water and fish that will be eaten by people. Mercury can cause birth defects, nerve disorders, and other health problems. By analyzing the distinctive chemical "fingerprint" of certain types of mercury, scientists in 2013 linked the rising levels of mercury in nine species of Pacific Ocean fish to coal-fired power plants in Asia, but the problem is not limited to Asia. The U.S. Environmental Protection Agency (EPA) points out that coal-fired power plants account for more than half of all human-caused mercury emissions into the air in the United States. U.S. coal-fired plants also produce more than 30 percent of the nation's carbon dioxide emissions, which are major contributors to climate change.

Can We Afford Clean Coal?

Coal has become cleaner since the 1970s, chiefly because laws such as the Clean Air Act and Clean Water Act, enforced by the EPA and by countless lawsuits against power companies brought by community and environmental organizations, have required companies that burned coal to adopt new technologies and methods to reduce pollutants. Coal is not pollution-free, however, and the question of whether coal can truly be a low-carbon emission fuel remains to be answered.

Carbon capture and storage technology (CCS) promises to remove carbon dioxide from coal exhaust before the exhaust is vented into the atmosphere, and the few CCS projects already in operation show that it

A DEEPER DIVE

The High Cost of Washing Coal

On January 9, 2014, a clear liquid that smelled like licorice leaked from a storage tank into the Elk River in West Virginia, a state with many coal mines. The liquid was the chemical 4-methylcyclohexane methanol, or MCHM. It is a type of detergent that is used to wash or treat coal after it has been mined, to separate it from unburnable materials such as shale, clay, and sand. Both the company that owned the leaking storage tank and the federal Food and Drug Administration admitted that MCHM's effects on human health and the environment are largely unknown. The spill contaminated water for 300,000 people in West Virginia, including residents of the capital, Charleston. Government and health officials issued warnings against drinking, bathing with, or washing dishes or clothing in the water. Trucks brought in hundreds of thousands of bottles of water for people unable to use the water from their faucets. Even after the water was pronounced safe, however, long-term testing will still be needed to monitor water quality and to check for contamination of the riverbanks and the ground around the storage facility.

It took just twenty minutes for this water truck to be emptied in Charleston, West Virginia, after a disastrous chemical leak in January 2014 made local water unusable.

An artist's vision of the FutureGen power plant, which critics call a costly mistake.

can be done. Several large issues remain. Will CCS be cost effective—that is, will the benefits and profits from continuing to burn coal into the future be greater than the costs of the technology? Is it safe to store huge quantities of carbon dioxide underground?

The question of cost-effectiveness is hard to answer. Whenever a new technology is introduced, the development and start-up costs are much higher than the costs of duplicating the technology later on. The cost of the FutureGen project to develop a CCS coal-burning plant in Illinois has been estimated at $1.65 billion, but it will almost certainly cost more if it is ever completed. The Kemper Project, a high-technology coal mine and power plant with CCS being built in Mississippi, was originally expected to cost $2.8 billion, but as of late 2013 costs for the project were revised upward to $5 billion. Governments and power companies, of course, pass their costs on to citizens in the form of taxes, bonds, and electricity rate increases. For now, the building of coal-fired plants that meet the emissions-control needs of the future remains an extremely costly business.

What about the long-term safety of storing carbon dioxide or injecting it into the ground? Carbon storage is fairly new and has not yet been widely tested. The biggest potential problem is leakage from

A DEEPER DIVE

Pea-Soupers

Concerns about the negative effects of coal are not new. By the nineteenth century, coal had given rise to a highly unpleasant feature of city life: the extremely heavy yellow, green, or brown smogs that English people called "pea-soupers" because they were said to be "as thick as pea soup." Fed by the smoke from thousands of home and industrial fireplaces burning soft coal, these smogs contained soot and chemicals such as sulfur dioxide. They occurred in many cities but were especially notable in London, where the smog combined with fog from the Thames River to form a thick, low-lying haze that made it hard to breathe or see. One of the worst recorded London pea-soupers was the four-day "Great Smog" of 1952. Afterward, British doctors estimated that this event contributed to four thousand premature deaths and a hundred thousand illnesses. Four years after the Great Smog, Britain passed its first Clean Air Act, which made it illegal to use soft coal for cooking and heating in urban homes.

storage facilities, reservoirs, or the trucks or pipelines used to carry the carbon dioxide to the reservoirs. Geophysicist Mark Zoback of Stanford University calls carbon capture "a risky, and likely unsuccessful, strategy" to limit global warming, saying that injecting gases into the ground in high quantities could trigger earthquakes, which even if small might cause the reservoirs to leak. Like much else about global climate change and the future of energy use, carbon capture is a subject of much debate and speculation.

Coal Is Not Forever

There is a lot of coal in the world, but it won't last forever. It might not even last the 112 years predicted by the World Coal Association. Suppose that all coal combustion were made as clean as it could possibly be, with the absolute minimum of pollutants and greenhouse gases emitted into the atmosphere. Would it then be a good idea to rely on coal for future energy? Some people say no.

Coal, like all fossil fuels, is finite. The world will one day run out of it. The answer to keeping our energy-guzzling civilization going without fossil fuels lies in other sources of power, such as nuclear and renewable energy—possibly including energy sources not yet discovered. The use of renewable energy is on the rise. Many believe that, at some point, the world will have to transition to a renewable-energy model. Rather than spending large sums to develop new ways of using fossils fuels, including coal, some energy planners want to see more research and development of renewable energy, or even safe nuclear energy. In their view, the high cost of coal lies not just in health and environmental damage, but in the resources coal takes away from other energy possibilities.

CRITICAL THINKING

- Closing coal-fueled electrical plants may lead to higher costs for electricity. How might that affect you? Would you be willing to pay more for electricity, or to reduce the amount of it you use, in order to cut down on the amount of electricity being generated from coal?

- Is it fair to ask people in the developing world—in countries such as India, China, and Indonesia, for example—not to aspire to the energy-rich lifestyle of the developed world in order to keep carbon emissions down?

- Are the operators of coal mines meeting their responsibilities to their employees and to the environment? Why or why not?

The Boardman plant in Oregon became a focus for questions about the role of coal in the nation's energy future.

Chapter 4

The Future of Coal

The town of Boardman sits on the bank of the Columbia River in eastern Oregon. A few miles south of town is a power plant that began operation under Portland General Electric (PGE) in 1977. By the early twenty-first century, the Boardman plant was Oregon's only coal-burning power plant—a source of inexpensive power for Oregonians, but also the state's top source of greenhouse gas emissions and air pollution. It was also the focus of negotiations between PGE, the state's Environmental Quality Commission (EQC), and environmental groups that include Greenpeace and the Sierra Club. The debate over the fate of the Boardman power plant stands as a symbol of the questions, concerns, and difficult decisions that will shape the future of coal.

Case History: The Boardman Power Plant

Boardman is neither the oldest nor the largest of the nation's coal-burning power plants. It is among the top third of plants nationwide in terms of efficiency. However, like every other power plant in the United States, Boardman is subject to the emissions standards and limits of the

Clean Air Act. After President Barack Obama took office in early 2009, the Environmental Protection Agency (EPA) began more strictly enforcing the Act's regulations that govern the emission of such pollutants as sulfur dioxide and nitrogen oxides, which create haze in the air. At the same time, it became increasingly likely that the EPA would soon put in place new regulations to govern greenhouse gas emissions such as carbon.

The Boardman plant emits 25,500 tons of pollutants and four million tons of greenhouse gases each year. In 2009, the EPA issued a violation notice to the plant, charging that it has operated since 1998 without adequate pollution controls. Several environmental groups sued PGE for failing to install a complete set of pollution controls when the plant was built, and activists clamored for the plant to be closed immediately. PGE pointed to the fact that closure would undoubtedly lead to higher electricity prices, along with the loss of 130 jobs.

At stake was not just the plant's immediate future but its long-term future. Experts calculated that to bring the Boardman plant into compliance with current laws, and then keep it operating in compliance through the year 2040, would require an investment of $500 million in pollution controls, such as upgraded equipment and new technology, just to meet current pollution standards. That did not take into account the fact that, in the future, standards could become stricter, which would require still more investments in the plant (in fact, in 2014 the EPA did publish proposed new rules for carbon emissions).

In 2010, the EQC announced that a deal had been made. In exchange for agreeing to stop burning coal at the Boardman plant by 2020, PGE was allowed to invest the much smaller sum of $50 million in pollution controls to keep the plant operating for another ten years. The deal made

Marchers demonstrate against pollution from a lignite-burning power plant in Australia in a protest similar to one against the pollution from Boardman.

Boardman the youngest coal plant in the United States to agree to early closure for environmental reasons. Meanwhile, local and county officials around Boardman hope that PGE, the Oregon Environmental Council, and other interested groups will work together to find a replacement for coal, such as natural gas, so that a greener, economically and environmentally satisfactory power plant can operate in the area.

As the Boardman case shows, decisions about coal-fired plants must take into consideration an array of concerns: pollution (present and future), economics (jobs lost, costs of bringing plants into compliance with regulations, price increases for electricity consumers, health costs due to pollution), the changing landscape of carbon regulation, and as EQC vice-chairman Ken Williamson pointed out right before the commission voted to accept the plan, the fact that "[W]e're all addicted to using a lot of electricity." The future of coal, both in the United States and abroad, will depend upon how governments, regulators, corporations, and citizens balance those concerns.

Coal's Ups and Downs

Coal has had its ups and downs since it shot to prominence during the Industrial Revolution. In terms of its share of the world's total energy use, coal hit its peak around 1910, according to Roy Neresian, author of *Energy for the 21st Century: A Comprehensive Guide to Conventional and Alternative Sources* (2010). At that time, coal contributed 60 percent of the world's energy. Another 30 percent came from the burning of biomass— wood, charcoal, and peat. The final 10 percent came from oil, natural gas, and hydropower, which is electricity generated from the energy of falling water at waterfalls or dams.

Things started to change after 1910. Oil rose in importance as the automobile, powered by gasoline refined from oil, took its place in modern life. Oil also replaced coal as the fuel of ocean-going ships because it required less labor to use—on the steamship *Titanic*, for example, 160 men shoveled 600 tons of coal each day into the furnaces that drove the ship.

Sweating stokers pile coal into a ship's boilers in the 1920s. Shipping companies soon shifted to oil as fuel.

After the 1920s, homeowners began to shift away from coal furnaces to heating systems powered by oil, propane, or natural gas. Coal cookstoves gave way to electric stoves or ones powered by propane or butane.

By the middle of the century, the primary uses for coal were as fuel sources for electrical plants and steam locomotives. Coal prices rose after a series of strikes organized by John L. Lewis, a coal miner who served as president of the United Mine Workers of America from 1920 to 1960,

A DEEPER DIVE

From Coal to Diamonds?
No Way!

Popular lore says that a lump of coal turns into a diamond when it is subjected to intense pressure, the kind of pressure that comes from spending millions of years buried in the Earth—or, according to comic books, from being crushed in Superman's super-strong hands. In reality, neither Superman nor the sheer passage of time is enough to turn a lump of coal into a diamond.

Coal and diamonds are both made of carbon, but that's where the similarity ends. Diamonds are pure, or nearly pure, carbon. Coal contains many elements in addition to carbon, including nitrogen, oxygen, hydrogen, sulfur, selenium, mercury, and arsenic. Coal may also contain complex carbon-based molecules left over from its time as living, then decaying, plant matter. The carbon in diamonds was never alive. It originated deep within Earth's mantle, the hot layer between the planet's outer crust and its inner core. The combination of intense

This antique German pin is made of jet, a gem carved from hard, shiny coal.

pressure and intense heat causes carbon atoms to bond in the crystalline form that, when it is finally brought to the surface by volcanic activity and erosion, we call a diamond.

One gemstone, though, is made from coal. Jet is a shiny black stone carved from certain varieties of coal. Known to the ancient Chinese and Romans, jet became especially popular in the nineteenth century, when it was often used in mourning jewelry to commemorate the dead, due to its somber color. Today, many pieces of jewelry called "jet" are really made of black glass or plastic. Unlike those materials, though, true jet does not feel cool to the touch.

The Pros and Cons of Coal

The oil crisis of 1973 was a rude awakening for Americans, who suddenly found themselves short of gasoline. In some states, drivers could buy gas only on certain days, depending upon whether their license plates were even- or odd-numbered.

succeeded in improving wages, pensions, and working conditions for miners. Rising coal prices encouraged the shift to oil, and the railroads, which had previously resisted changing from coal to diesel fuel (made from oil), now made the shift. Although new coal-fired power plants continued to be built after the middle of the century, plants using oil, natural gas, or nuclear power were also constructed.

Coal got a boost in 1973, when political and economic disputes caused a group of oil-producing nations, mostly in the Middle East, to halt their exports of oil. This led to an oil crisis in other parts of the world, including the United States.

People waited in long lines at gas stations to buy rationed fuel for their automobiles, and conservation measures such as turning off unused lights and lowering thermostats suddenly became normal behavior for many people. In terms of industrial fuels, coal suddenly looked more attractive. However, once the oil crisis ended in 1974, coal resumed its slow decline. In the 2000s, the use of new techniques for increasing oil and natural gas production in North America led to lower prices for those fuels, further chipping away at coal's status. By 2013, coal accounted for just 18.3 percent of the energy used in the United States and produced 37 percent of the country's electricity.

Looking Ahead

What does the future hold for coal? The coal industry hopes that new clean-coal technologies will support the use of coal, with its many advantages, into the future. Environmentalists generally hope to see coal phased out in favor of greener, renewable energy sources. Another perspective comes from the U.S. Energy Information Administration (EIA). This federal office gathers data and produces reports on energy production, use, and trends—both within the United States and around the world—that could affect the markets for U.S. energy.

In a report released in late 2013, the EIA described the state of the U.S. coal industry in 2012. The use of coal within the United States had decreased 3.5 percent from 2011. The coal mining industry employed 90,000 people, a decrease of almost 2 percent from 2011. It produced 1,016,458 tons of coal, a 7.2 percent drop in production from 2011 and the lowest in almost twenty years.

Wind power, generated from turbines, and solar power, collected from panels, are examples of renewable energy. Some critics of coal would rather see money devoted to this type of energy than to clean-coal projects.

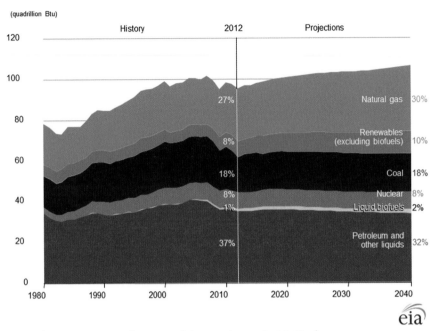

(quadrillion Btu)

History   2012   Projections

Natural gas 30%   27%

Renewables
(excluding biofuels) 10%   8%

Coal 18%   18%

Nuclear 8%   8%

Liquid biofuels 2%   1%

Petroleum and
other liquids 32%   37%

eia

Projected energy use in the United States through 2040 shows
coal use remaining stable.

The EIA also charted energy use in the United States by type of fuel,
using historical data since 1980 and projections of future use through
2040. The EIA expects that coal use will remain steady at around
18 percent of total energy use through 2040, assuming that current laws
and regulations remain in force. Petroleum fuels, in comparison, are
expected to lose a bit of the energy pie, declining from 37 percent in
2012 to 32 percent in 2040, while natural gas will increase from 27 to
30 percent and renewable energy sources will increase from 8 to 10
percent in the same period. As for generating electricity, the primary use of
coal today, the EIA expects that natural gas' contribution to total electricity
generation will increase from 30 percent in 2012 to 35 percent in 2040,

renewables' share will rise from 12 to 16 percent, and coal's will fall from 37 to 32 percent—after having reached a high of 52 percent in 2000.

In short, the EIA expects coal use in the United States to remain more or less unchanged overall through 2040, although as the amount of electricity generated goes up, coal will contribute a smaller percentage of total electrical production. Trends in plant construction and closure seem to reinforce the idea that coal use will not grow. Although planning was under way in the early 2000s for approximately 120 new coal-fired power plants across the United States, most of those plans have been dropped. And Oregon's Boardman plant is not the only one to have announced an early closure. As of early 2014, about 30 percent of all U.S. coal-fired power plants had either closed or announced that they would be closing in the near future.

Coal use is on the rise—sometimes dramatically—in other parts of the world, however. "World coal consumption grew by 59 percent from 2000 to 2010," says the EIA, "largely because of China's rapidly growing energy demand. In China alone, coal consumption tripled over the 2000–2010 period."

In 2010, three nations accounted for 70 percent of the world's total coal use. They were China (47 percent), the United States (14 percent), and India (9 percent). Energy forecasters expect that by 2040—if current trends and emissions regulations remain unchanged—those same nations will consume 75 percent of all the coal used in the world.

China is, and will remain, the world's biggest coal user. According to the EIA, "China alone contributed 88 percent of the growth in world coal consumption from 2001 to 2009." The EIA predicts that China's percentage of total world coal use will rise to 57 percent by 2025, then

A DEEPER DIVE

China's Smog Problem

In the middle of January 2014, a thick yellow smog filled the air in Beijing, the capital of China. The city's atmosphere contained more than twenty times the level of pollutants that the World Health Organization considers safe. Some highways were temporarily closed, and the people of Beijing, especially children and old people, were advised to stay indoors. Tianjin and other cities in the region were also blanketed with dangerously thick smog—and it wasn't the first time.

China's capital and other major cities have suffered from extremely high levels of air pollution in recent years. Automobile exhaust from the ever-increasing number of cars in China is part of the problem, but one major cause of smog and air pollution is the burning of coal to heat homes and to power industry. Air quality is worst in winter, when home furnaces receive their heaviest use. The mayor of Beijing announced that coal use would be

reduced in and around the city. The Chinese government has also announced plans to lower its projected coal use by as much as 5 percent between now and the middle of the century. It remains to be seen whether China's efforts to limit the use of fossil fuels at the city and the national levels will succeed and improve the country's air quality.

India is one of the world's fastest-growing users of coal. The demand for electricity leads to frequent power shortages in many parts of the country.

The Pros and Cons of Coal

decline slightly to 55 percent by 2040. India, meanwhile, is expected to pass the United States and become the second-largest user of coal by 2030. Overall, coal is expected to contribute a quarter of the world's total energy through 2040, and to generate more than a third of its electricity. As for the more distant future, most forecasters think that coal use will remain flat or slowly decline after the middle of the century.

Although the use of most other forms of energy is rising faster than coal use, coal will not disappear from the world's energy mix any time soon. In fact, coal production—the mining and shipping of coal—will increase from 8 billion tons in 2010 to 11.5 billion tons in 2040. Since the combination of environmental concerns and lower natural gas prices is driving a shift away from coal use in North America, the increase in coal use will be greater in other nations. Coal exports from the United States to other countries have risen significantly from 50 million tons in 2005 to an all-time high of 126 million tons in 2012. In Europe, in particular, rising natural gas prices have brought an increase in the use of coal imported from the United States. Overseas, China's coal use is expected to become more efficient as advanced new power plants replace older ones; China will also build more nuclear, natural gas, and hydropower plants to provide electricity. India, which is expected to have a larger population than China by the 2020s, will continue to rely heavily on coal to provide electricity to meet the demands of its growing middle class, even though other power sources are also expected to grow in the country.

Coal was the first fuel of humankind's industrial age. As an energy source it offers both unique advantages and grave disadvantages. Coal's fortunes have risen and fallen over the years due to factors such as competition from other energy sources, shortages of other fuels, and

A coal-fired power plant in Shuozhou, China, forms part of the energy mix in a nation that has seen rapid growth of industry. China is also investing in hydropower and natural gas plants.

environmental concerns. In the future, unforeseen circumstances or technological advances could bring another swift rise in coal's fortunes, especially if it becomes economically efficient to maintain strict control of pollution and carbon emissions from coal-burning power plants. More likely, however, this ancient fuel will continue to be one piece of the world's increasingly complex energy mix, gradually giving way to other energy sources in some parts of the world—but elsewhere remaining vitally important for growth.

CRITICAL THINKING

- Would the world be a better or worse place today if people had decided not to use coal for energy? Why?

- Should coal play a larger or a smaller role in the energy future of the United States and the world? Why?

anthracite: the hardest, driest, and most energy-rich form of coal; the highest rank of coal

bituminous: coal that is softer and contains more moisture than anthracite; there are several ranks of bituminous and sub-bituminous coal between anthracite and lignite.

brown coal: another name for lignite, the lowest rank of coal

carbon capture and storage (CCS): also referred to as carbon capture and sequestration, this refers to proposed methods of removing carbon dioxide (and other greenhouse gases) from the exhaust created by burning coal, then storing those gases underground or in a secure way instead of letting them enter the atmosphere

clean coal technologies (CCT): devices or processes aimed at making energy from coal more efficient and less polluting

coke: fuel produced by baking coal to burn off moisture and impurities

fossil fuel: fuel formed from long-buried remains of ancient plant or animal life: coal, oil, and natural gas

greenhouse gas: any gas that traps heat in Earth's atmosphere and contributes to the warming of the planet; one of the most significant greenhouse gases is carbon dioxide, released when coal is burned

impurities: elements in coal that keep it from being pure carbon, such as water, arsenic, sulfur, and other materials

integrated gasification combined cycle (IGCC): coal-burning process in which the coal is transformed into gas before being burned, and impurities, pollutants and carbon dioxide are removed before combustion

lignite or **brown coal:** the softest and most moisture-filled coal; the lowest rank of coal

overburden: layers of soil and rock that must be scraped or blasted away to expose a seam of coal in surface mining

peat: fuel in the form of compressed, partially decayed vegetation; it forms in bogs and other wetlands and is cut out in blocks, pressed, and dried before burning

piston: a solid shaft that moves up and down inside a hollow tube or cylinder, pushed by expanding gases or steam, or pulled by a vacuum; turns the energy of steam or heated gas into power through a bar attached to the top of the piston to drive machinery

renewable energy: any type of energy, such as solar or wind power, that does not depend on fuels that exist in limited amounts and can be used only once

reserve: amount of a resource that can be recovered using current technology and under current regulations

Find Out More

Books

Espejo, Roman, ed. *Coal*. Opposing Viewpoints Series. Farmington Hills, MI: Greenhaven, 2011.

Morgan, Sally. *Oil, Gas, and Coal*. New York, NY: Hodder Wayland, 2009.

Parks, Peggy J. *Coal Power*. San Diego, CA: Referencepoint Press, 2010.

Websites

Coal
www.eia.gov/coal

The U.S. Energy Information Administration maintains a webpage of news and statistics about the coal industry in the United States. It provides official data on how much coal is mined, used, and exported, as well as forecasts for the future

Coal Energy Facts

teachcoal.org/coal-energy-facts

The American Coal Foundation's website has a page of fast facts about coal, as well as articles about coal mining and the environment and the history of coal in America.

Coal Is Dirty and Dangerous

www.nrdc.org/energy/coalnotclean.asp

The Natural Resources Defense Council presents reasons not to use coal, including arguments that "clean coal" is a myth.

Unacceptable Risk: The Real Price of Coal Mining

www.popularmechanics.com/science/energy/coal-oil-gas/real-price-of-coal-mining-investigative-report

A report from *Popular Mechanics* argues that coal mining operations are too dangerous to workers.

Page numbers in **boldface** are illustrations.

anthracite, 38, **39**
augers, 32

Bessemer, Henry, 18
bituminous, 38, **39**
black lung, 20
Boardman power plant, **54**, 55–58
brown coal, 37
    see also lignite
Bruce, Sir George, 14

carbon capture and storage (CCS), **28**, 37, 40, 47, 50
Carboniferous period, 6–7
"choke damp," 22
clean coal technologies, (CCT), 29, 34–36, 64

coal
    advantages of, 29–40
    converted to electricity, 5, 19, 29, 35, 50, 53, 56, 58, 64, 66–67, **70**, 71
    disadvantages of, 43–52
    early uses, 7–13
    future of, 64–72
    in the Industrial Revolution, 5, 13–19, 27, 58
    mines and miners, 19–26, 32–33
    origins of, 5–6
coke, 7, 17–18

Department of Energy, 30, 37, 40

Environmental Protection Agency (EPA), 47, 56

"fire damp," 22
fossil fuel, 27, 29, 37, 43, 52, 69
FutureGen, 40, **50**

Rebecca Stefoff has written many books on science, technology, the environment, and social issues for young readers. Recent publications include the four-volume Animal Behavior Revealed series (Cavendish Square, 2014), the six-volume Is It Science? series (Cavendish Square, 2014), Managing Land Use (Cavendish Square, 2012), and the four-volume series Humans: An Evolutionary History (Cavendish Square, 2009). Learn more about Stefoff and her books for young people at www.rebeccastefoff.com.